GET A

OLIVER CROMWELL

Books in the GET A LIFE! series

William the Conqueror
Elizabeth I
Julius Caesar
Florence Nightingale
Henry VIII
Queen Victoria
Oliver Cromwell
Marie Curie
Napoleon
Mary Queen of Scots

GET A LIFE!
OLIVER CROMWELL

PHILIP ARDAGH

Illustrated by Alan Rowe

MACMILLAN CHILDREN'S BOOKS

For Martin Roxbee Cox,
who'd ban Christmas too,
for the turkeys' sake.

First published 2000
by Macmillan Children's Books
a division of Macmillan Publishers Ltd
25 Eccleston Place, London SW1W 9NF
Basingstoke and Oxford
www.macmillan.co.uk

Associated companies throughout the world

ISBN 0 330 37572 5

1 3 5 7 9 8 6 4 2

A CIP catalogue record for this book is available from the British Library.

Printed by Mackays of Chatham plc, Chatham, Kent.

CONTENTS

Family Tree 6

Useful Words 7

Little Ollie 9

[Un]Civil War! 26

The Fight Continues 46

The Lord Protector 54

Timeline 64

The Author's Rather Weedy

FAMILY TREE

(Well More of a Shrub Really)

OF OLIVER CROMWELL

with loads of unfortunate folk left out

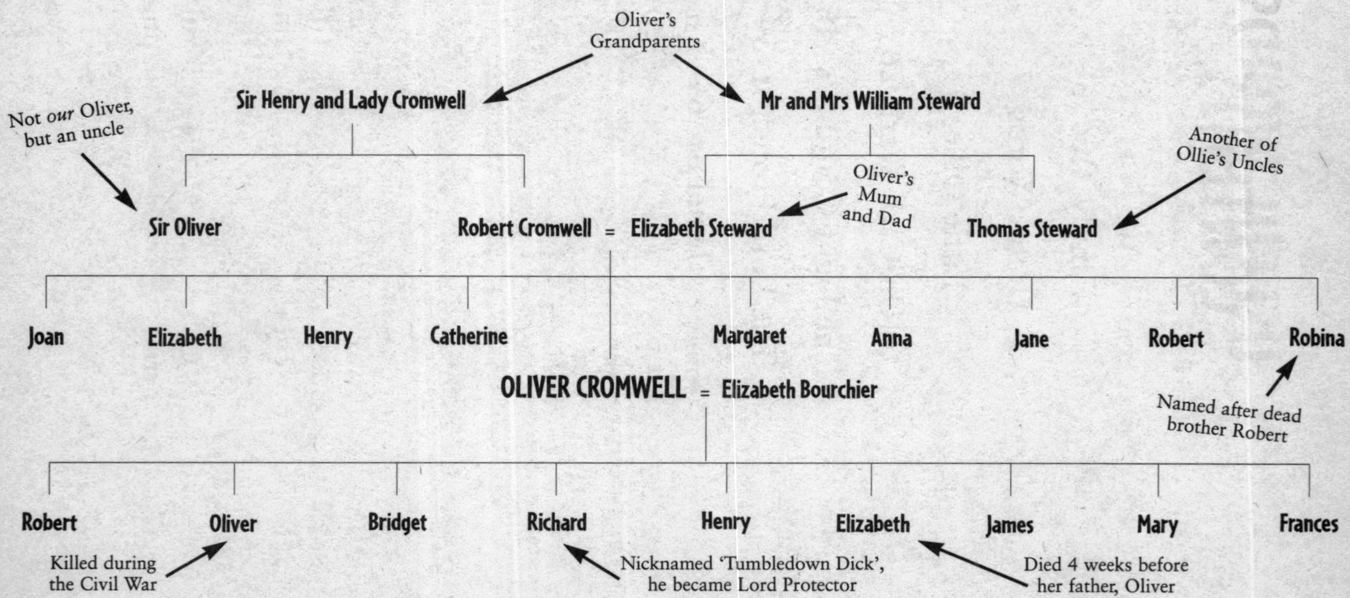

USEFUL WORDS

(Some jolly useful and others useful but not jolly at all)

Behead Chop someone's head off. (Being beheaded is having your head chopped off.) A bit like pruning, except you don't grow a new head the following year.

Cavaliers Royalists. In other words, the people who supported the royals, as in His *Royal* Highness, the king.

Cavalry Horse-riding soldiers and their horses too, I suppose.

Commoner Someone who wipes his or her nose on his or her sleeve. Not really. It's a person who isn't a member of the nobility (who are people with posh titles such as Duke or Earl).

Commonwealth Today, the Commonwealth is a group of nations that are, or used to be, governed by Britain. In Cromwell's day it meant something completely different: the British republic from 1649 to 1660.

Maiden name When a woman marries, she often drops her surname and uses her husband's instead (though not always nowadays, of course). Her maiden name is her original surname.

Martial Law Governing by military rules, without civil rights or civil trials. In other words treating ordinary people like soldiers.

Musketeer A soldier armed with a musket. (Obvious, huh?)

Musket A weapon carried by a musketeer. (Tee-hee!) Actually, it's a long-barrelled rifle. Between each firing, the shot (ammunition) had to be poured down the end of the barrel with the gunpowder.

Pike A freshwater fish . . . but that's not the kind of pike you'll read about in this book. Here, it's a long pole (a pikestaff) with a steel spearhead on the end. Very pointy. Very painful.

Republic A country, nation or state ruled by an elected government, not a king or queen . . . even if it means getting rid of one first.

Roundheads The parliamentarians – supporters of parliament, not the king.

Rout To force or drive out. A great word to use when describing one army seeing off another.

LITTLE OLLIE

Oliver Cromwell is one of the most hated men in British history. He was on the winning side in the English Civil War of 1642, which saw an end to the British monarchy . . . though only for a little while. (In case you hadn't noticed, Britain still has a monarch on the throne today. It's another word for king or queen.) He was behind the beheading of King Charles I and the banning of the celebration of Christmas. But that's only one version of events. Cromwell – and Mrs Cromwell – probably thought he was one of the good guys . . .

ONE IN TEN

Oliver Cromwell was born in England on 25 April 1599, in a place called Huntingdon, in the county of Huntingdonshire. (No one lives in the county any more. Not because it's radioactive

or anything, it's just that a number of county boundaries were changed in 1974 and Huntingdonshire disappeared from the map.) Oliver's grandfather, Sir Henry, and uncle both lived in Hinchinbrook, a big house nearby. Oliver's parents, Robert and Elizabeth had TEN children altogether. Oliver was their fifth child and second son. Only seven children lived to be grown-ups, and Oliver was the only boy.

OF ROYAL BLOOD

Oliver's mum, Elizabeth, had been Elizabeth *Lynne* when she'd first met Oliver's dad, but Lynne wasn't her maiden name. That was Steward. She'd been married to a Mr William Lynne but he had died, along with their only child. The interesting thing about the Stewards is that many experts (with huge domed foreheads to make room for all those brains) believe that they were descended from the *royal* Stuarts of Scotland. So it's rather funny (sick) that Oliver Cromwell, who later helped behead a Stuart king and abolish the monarchy, had some royal blood – even from the same *family* – in his veins!

GRANDPA DIES

Oliver was just under four when his grandfather, Sir Henry Cromwell, died in January 1603. This was the same year that King James VI of Scotland came down to England to become King James I of England too. (These numbers may seem a bit confusing. All it means is that he was the sixth James to be king in Scotland, but only the first James to be king in England. Clear? Good.) He stayed in Hinchinbrook, which had been Sir Henry's house but which now belonged to Oliver's uncle (his father's elder brother, who inherited all the goodies when Grandpa died). His uncle showered the new king with gifts and, in return, King James made him a knight. Another person to be made a knight by the king was Oliver's other uncle – his mum's brother – Thomas Steward. So little Oliver had 'Sirs' on both sides of the family.

THE WORTHY DR BEARD

Oliver was taught at the local school in Huntingdon and that meant being taught by Dr Thomas Beard. Whether the doctor actually had a beard, we don't know. It would be nice to think so, though. Dr Beard was a doctor of divinity (religion) and when he wasn't teaching he was preaching . . . which sounds a bit like the words to a song. There were two churches in the town – All Saints and St John's (where Oliver was baptized) – which was on the bank of the River Ouse, looking across the marshy Fens.

TO CAMBRIDGE . . . BUT NOT FOR LONG

On 23 April 1616 (just two days before his seventeenth birthday, and the day that William Shakespeare's said to have died) Oliver started at Sidney Sussex College, Cambridge University. In June of the following year, Oliver's father Robert died. His remaining grandfather (his mother's father) also died. Oliver had to give up university life because he was suddenly responsible for looking after his mother and his unmarried sisters. There then followed one of those gaps which mystery writers love so much, because they can make up loads of stories about what went on, and no one really knows what's true and what isn't!

INN OR OUT?

One theory is that Oliver went to London to one of the 'inns of court' to train to be a lawyer . . . but, although there are written records surviving from those days, none contain Oliver Cromwell's name. The conclusion? That he didn't go to Lincoln's Inn, Gray's Inn or any other London Inn of

Court, whatever anyone might have thought. He probably went to get a taste for the law by working in the chambers (offices) of some lawyer, but never actually trained. Rumours that he had a wild time up in London can't be proven either.

A NEW FAMILY

Oliver Cromwell married Elizabeth – no, not his mum, another Elizabeth with the maiden name Bourchier – on 22 August 1620. How they met, we don't know, but we do know that they got married in St Giles's Church, Cripplegate in London. Oliver was 21 years old and took his new wife back to his house in Huntingdon where his mum and (maybe) some of his sisters lived. We also know that most of the Cromwell girls were either married or thinking of marrying by now. Oliver and Elizabeth's first child, a son, was born in October 1621. They named him Robert, after Oliver's dead father, and had him baptized in St John's as Oliver himself had been. He died before he was eighteen, and was the first of nine children. Another son was born in February 1623, about whom jolly little is known. We do know that Oliver Cromwell farmed the land surrounding his property.

A CHANGE OF BELIEFS

At some time during this period, Oliver became a Calvinist. In those days, most people in Britain were Christian, but there were many different types of Christian, as you can see in the next section, headed ALL SHAPES AND SIZES. Calvinists followed the teachings of John Calvin. A Frenchman, he was the leader of the Protestant Reformation in France and Switzerland. Calvinists wore very simple clothes and wanted worship to be a serious no-frills business, and certainly not fun.

ALL SHAPES AND SIZES

Until Henry VIII broke away in the 1530s, England's official faith was Roman Catholicism. Its leader, the Pope, was (and still is) seen as God's Representative on Earth. Roman Catholicism is seen as 'High Church' with plenty of statues and incense and praying to saints. Protestants are really any Christians who aren't Roman Catholics. England's new official faith became Church of England (or Anglicanism) with the king or queen as its head. Another kind of Protestantism is Puritanism. Puritans were a bunch of 'Low Church' Protestants who believed that everything should be plain and humble. There were many other types of Protestant too, including the Episcopalians, Quakers and the Presbyterians (and you'll be reading a lot about Presbyterians) . . . but don't forget, these were all simply different types of Christian.

TO PARLIAMENT

In March 1628, Oliver became the member of parliament for Huntingdon. In other words, he was an MP and went to Westminster in London to sit in the House of Commons in the Houses of Parliament. (It wasn't the same building we have today with Big Ben and all that, though.) James VI of Scotland and I of England had died in 1625 and his son Charles was now King Charles I.

(Charles had an elder brother, Henry, but Henry had died way back in 1612.) The parliament Oliver Cromwell sat in was Charles's third. The king had dismissed the first two because they didn't do what he wanted them to do . . . fair enough, I suppose!!!

THE PETITION OF RIGHT

If Charles thought that he'd be in for an easier time with this third parliament than the other two, he was sadly mistaken! This new parliament was mainly made up of men with a strong Puritanical belief in God's law and the word of the Gospel. (Yes, that's 'Puritanical' as in 'Puritan' as in NO FUN.) They insisted on passing the Petition of Right. In the past, Charles I had thrown those people who wouldn't fund his war with France into prison without charge or trial . . . and wouldn't let them out. The Petition of Right declared that being imprisoned without proper cause, raising taxes without parliament's consent, and putting people under martial (military) law were all illegal.

THE THIRTY YEARS' WAR

Even when Charles's father, King James I, was still alive, a religious war – called the Thirty Years' War – was raging in Europe, mainly on German soil. It was a war of Protestant countries (and France) against the Habsburg Empire and Spain, who wanted Germany to be ruled by Catholic kings. James wanted England to be on the right side of as many people as possible, so he made his daughter marry a German prince. Charles was persuaded to marry the sister of France's Catholic king in 1625. Her name was Henrietta Maria and she was only fifteen. The wedding was in Notre Dame Cathedral in Paris, but Charles didn't even turn up. He got his mate, the Duke of Buckingham, to stand in for him! So the duke took all the vows on his behalf. Not that it made much difference, France was soon an enemy again anyway. The Thirty Years' War lasted from 1618 to 1648. In the end, the Germans came off worst and the French best.

CELEBRATION!

The acceptance of the Petition of Right was greeted with the ringing of bells and the building of bonfires in London. This was a great victory for parliament and an embarrassment for the king. Charles hastily 'prorogued' parliament. This meant that he was sending parliament off on holiday without actually scrapping it. Oliver Cromwell returned to Huntingdon until January, when parliament reassembled.

MORE SKIRMISHES WITH HIS MAJESTY

Back in business, parliament ran headlong into another argument with the king. Charles I had been able to raise 'tonnage and poundage' on goods coming in and out of the country – what we talk about as 'customs and excise duties' today – without having to agree the amounts with parliament. If he wanted more money, he simply put up the tonnage and poundage and the poor old merchants simply had to pay. The Members of Parliament argued that this was now covered by the taxation part of the Petition of Right . . . especially because some merchants had been imprisoned by the king for non-payment.

TROUBLE BREWS

Another of this parliament's big gripes were the priests and bishops who were, in their eyes, a disgrace to the Church – men who seemed more interested in money, comfortable living and sucking up to the king than in behaving like true Christians. As a result, a Grand Committee of Religion was formed by parliament. It was in the meeting of one of these committees that, on 11 February 1629, Oliver Cromwell stood up and made his first speech in parliament.

MAIDEN SPEECH

In Oliver's speech, he quoted his old teacher Dr Beard and named two 'offending' churchmen. Oliver claimed that one Dr Alabaster had preached 'popery at Paul's Cross' and that the Bishop of Winchester had backed him! 'Popery' was another word for Roman Catholicism and was considered a very bad thing by parliament! Oliver Cromwell's allegations caused real shock. The Bishop supported the king and – surprise, surprise – less than two weeks later, Charles had dissolved parliament again. He carried on without one for ELEVEN years.

A COUNTRY WITHOUT PARLIAMENT

The country was now divided. There were those who supported the king and his 'high (almost-Catholic-but-not-quite) Anglicanism', and those who supported the rights and the laws of the people . . . but without a parliament to put forward their cause. Not only that, no one was even allowed to protest about the lack of parliament even if they wanted to. There was a royal proclamation forbidding it! Charles believed in 'the Divine Right of Kings'. In other words, he believed that God had given him the right to rule so he – Charles, not God – could do as he pleased, and no one could argue with him. It was God's will. Away from London, Oliver Cromwell was still actively involved in the community. He was a Justice of the Peace (a local judge), as was his old schoolmaster Dr Beard.

AN UNPOPULAR KING

Over the years, Charles I had done a number of things to make himself unpopular with all sorts of people. For example, at one stage, anyone who earned more than £40 off their land each year had to buy an expensive knighthood from him. It didn't matter if you wanted to be a 'Sir' or not. You HAD to buy one! Other land, he simply took from people saying that it was really his by right! One of his most wildly unpopular ideas – especially in a country with so much coastline – was 'Ship Money'. If you lived in a county with a coastline, you had to help pay for the upkeep of the navy!

PERSECUTION OF THE PURITANS

King Charles I had it in for the Puritans. These English Protestants, who were so 'low church' that they made the Anglicans seem Catholic, were given a tough time by one of the king's right-hand men, Archbishop Laud, the Archbishop of Canterbury. Some of these Puritans had had enough and, in 1630, a group of them set sail to start new lives in America. The most famous of these ships was the *Mayflower*. The people on board became known as the Pilgrim Fathers. This was a bit unfair on all the WOMEN who were on board and had sailed just as far. Perhaps it would be fairer to call them the Pilgrim *Parents* instead.

MOVING ON

In 1631, Oliver sold up his house and land in Huntingdon and moved too . . . but not to America. No, Oliver moved 5 miles down river to a place called St Ives. Here, he rented land to graze his livestock. The following year, 1632, saw the birth of Oliver and Elizabeth's seventh child. Baptized James, he died the next day. This left them with six children: Robert, Oliver, Bridget, Richard, Henry and Elizabeth. (Robert was to die young too, remember.) After James's death, they were to have two more children, Mary and Frances – a total of nine children, seven of whom lived long enough to become grown-ups.

TO ELY THEN TO LONDON

The year 1635 saw Oliver moving again, this time to Ely, home of his maternal uncle, Sir Thomas Steward, who had died. Here he added to his uncle's land by leasing other smaller fields, and continued to farm. He stayed there until the 'Long Parliament' of 1640 opened, which you can read about soon. To be close to the Houses of Parliament, he moved down to London. Elizabeth and his family stayed in Ely until it became obvious that, this time, parliament wasn't about to be cut short. The whole family upped and moved down to London in about 1647.

A VERY SHORT PARLIAMENT . . .

In 1640, King Charles decided that he needed to summon a parliament to raise money for an English army to fight the Scots, even though he'd actually been crowned King of

Scotland in 1633! The trouble was, he'd introduced a new English prayer book – which was unpopular enough with some of the English – and now he was trying to force it on the Scots. Many Scottish Presbyterians and Puritans had rebelled against it . . . and the king needed cash to fight them. So, on 13 April, the new parliament met, and Oliver was MP for Cambridge. As was now a familiar pattern, parliament didn't do what the king wanted so, on 5 May, he dismissed it in what a nineteenth-century historian, Thomas Carlyle, described as 'a huff', and I can't put it better than that.

. . . AND A VERY LONG ONE

Still in need of an army to fight the Scottish rebels, Charles raised the money without parliament's help. He forced people into giving him 'loans' and sent an army of foot soldiers to the Scottish borders. The Scots, meanwhile, were sending a rebel army into England. These Scots were Puritans and Presbyterians, as were many of the English soldiers who were supposed to be fighting them. They had more in common with each other than with the king! Charles I decided that the best thing was to have a peace treaty as soon as possible . . . so created yet another parliament. Little did he realize that this parliament would last for over twelve years and, known as the Long Parliament, become one of the most famous in British history.

GOOD LORD, LAUD!

One of the first things that the Long Parliament – in which our Oliver was an MP for Cambridge, remember – wanted was to get its power back. Charles I had been so used to doing things on his own without parliament, that they were eager to get some control again. They arranged for the arrest of Archbishop Laud who, amongst other things, had ordered the ears to be chopped off three men who'd dared give out pamphlets which criticized the king. (Some say that one man had already had his ears cut off for some previous offence and then had them sewn back on. It would have been the sewn-back-on-ears that were cut off this time!) Once arrested, parliament made the king sign the archbishop's death warrant, along with that of another powerful friend, the Earl of Stafford. Laud was imprisoned in the Tower of London for four years before being beheaded.

THE GRAND REMONSTRANCE

In November 1641, members of the House of Commons in the Long Parliament voted 'a Grand Remonstrance' against King Charles I. This was really a protest vote, but was only passed by a small majority. (In other words, a lot of MPs voted against the idea of a Grand Remonstrance, but a few more voted for it.) This stopped bishops and archbishops having so much power in the day-to-day running of the country, ordered a complete reformation of the church and – and this is one big AND, believe me – they put the army and navy under the control of parliament, not the king! Charles was horrified at what was happening and decided that he must DO something. He got together a group of soldiers, burst into the House of Commons and tried to arrest the leader of the house (a chap called John Pym) and his sidekicks . . . but they ran away and went and hid!

ROUNDHEADS AND CAVALIERS

In December 1641, a group of soldiers were on their way home after having had supper with King Charles I, when they were attacked by a bunch of apprentices – lads learning a trade. The apprentices were probably a bit drunk and just looking for a fight, and both sides started calling the other side names. The soldiers called the apprentices 'Roundheads' because of their short haircuts. (They, on the other hand – or should that be on the other head? – had long, flowing curls.) The apprentices called them 'Cavalieros' back, which was the name for the Catholic soldiers of Spain – based on the same word as 'cavalry' – one of the English Protestants' greatest enemies. 'Cavalieros' became 'Cavaliers' and the nicknames stuck. That's how supporters of parliament became known as Roundheads and supporters of the king (in other words, royalists) became

Cavaliers . . . At least, that's the traditional story of how the names came about, but you don't have to believe everything you read.

[UN]CIVIL WAR!

War was brewing, and a particularly nasty kind of war at that. This wasn't going to be one of those so-called 'glorious' wars when a country united and went off to fight some rotten foreigners. (This was at a time when everyone everywhere was a rotten foreigner to someone somewhere else!) No, this was going to be a *civil* war. If you've nothing better to do and look up 'civil' in a dictionary, you'll find it says something like 'polite or courteous'. Well, civil wars aren't polite or courteous. They're wars between people of the same country or nation. The war brewing in England would be between supporters of King Charles I and supporters of parliament. As with most wars, the ordinary 'I'm-not-sure-who's-right-or-wrong' folk would be stuck in the middle of it all. Most *un*civil, in fact.

THE KING'S MEN – CAVALIERS

When historians look up from their big, dusty books long enough to mention 'parliamentarians', they really mean members of the House of Commons and their supporters. The other house in the Houses of Parliament was, and still is – at the moment, anyway, but that could change very soon – the House of Lords. The House of Lords was full of . . . Go on, have a guess. (The clue is in the name: House of L-O-R-D-S.) Yes! It was full of *lords*. In other words, barons, dukes, earls, bishops and loads of other old fuddy-duddies who supported the king. Charles I also got support from the Roman Catholics and the north, including his stronghold in York. Another royalist stronghold was the south-west, that sticky-out part of England including Somerset, Devon and Cornwall and other places where they now do brilliant cream teas and make excellent ice cream.

CROMWELL'S LOT – THE ROUNDHEADS

The parliamentarians were actually led by a lord, the Earl of Essex. He was very rich and very popular and, along with the support of most of the members of the House of Commons (including our man Oliver Cromwell), he was also supported by the Puritans (who were always being given a rough ride by the king). These Roundheads had much wider support than the king. Most people in industrial areas, where jobs were grimy and low-paid, supported the Roundheads. Much of the south was pro-parliament too, and that included London.

A PLACE OF SAFETY

On 9 March 1642, Charles I put his wife on his warship, *The Lion*, docked at Dover so that she could sail away to safety . . . and, oh yes, so that she could pawn the Crown Jewels in Holland to get some money for him to buy weapons (and hand out a few smaller jewels to bribe a few others into supporting her husband, along the way). Oliver Cromwell, meanwhile, was giving his own money and time to the Roundhead cause. In February, he'd given money – some say £300, others say £500 or more – to help the Protestant Irish whom he saw as being persecuted by the Roman Catholic Irish in an Irish rebellion. In July, he raised an army of locals in his home county of Cambridge, prepared to defend it . . . presumably against the Cavaliers.

THIS MAGAZINE IS MINE, SIR

On 15 August (we're still in 1642) Oliver Cromwell became a real hero of the Roundheads. He seized 'the magazine' of the castle at Cambridge. OK, let's get the magazine jokes out of the way as quickly as possible. What I'm NOT talking about here is a magazine as in *Favourite Authors*

Monthly, a glossy 64-page periodical packed with amazing facts about wonderful authors such as Philip Ardagh. No, no, no. What I mean by the magazine of the castle at Cambridge is the building used to store all the weapons. These were weapons intended for the *king's* army. Now they were Cromwell's.

STEALING THE SILVER

As if that weren't enough, our Oliver then pulled off another stunt which made him rather popular with his fellow parliamentarians. Cambridge University had promised Charles I pile upon pile of silver plates which he could either eat off (unlikely) or sell to buy weapons (far more likely). It was valued at over £20,000 which was VERY BIG BUCKS in those days . . . and Oliver stopped it reaching the king. He decided that he'd hand it over to the Roundhead cause instead!

WAR!

Everyone knew that war was coming – except, perhaps, for a few village idiots, whose job it was to not know anything about anything – but when it was finally declared on 22 August 1642, nothing happened. The king had left London, where most Londoners didn't like him anyway. Records written in September 1642 list Oliver Cromwell, honourable Member of Parliament for Cambridge, as being the captain of Troop Sixty-Seven. The Roundhead army, under the command of the Duke of Essex's right-hand man, the Earl of Bedford, was divided into 75 troops with 60 men in each. Each troop had a captain in charge, a lieutenant as his number one – there were no *hers* in the army back then – a quartermaster in charge of provisions (that's food, uniforms and just about everything else), and someone called a cornet . . . and no ice cream jokes please. A cornet was the lowest rank of commissioned cavalry officer. Low it may have been, but you were still an officer, you were still commissioned (instead of coming from the real 'lower' ranks of ordinary soldiers) and, just as importantly, you still got to ride a horse. In Troop Eight, that position went to another Oliver Cromwell – our Oliver's son. It makes you proud, doesn't it?

THE ARMIES DRAW NEAR

The first battle of the English Civil War came about more by accident than design. Both the King's army and the Roundhead army were heading for London. The Roundhead army was ahead but, being bigger and better equipped, moved more slowly. The Cavaliers, who were fewer in number and had far fewer provisions, were beginning to catch up with them. Some Cavaliers went ahead of the main royalist forces to try to find food and lodgings for the army . . . and ran slap bang into some Roundheads doing the same in the village of Wormleighton! The Cavaliers thought this was too good an opportunity to miss, and took them prisoner.

A BATTLE, AND ABOUT TIME TOO

The Battle of Edgehill was fought in Warwickshire near a place called Keinton, which is why some people used to call it the Keinton Fight. It took place on 23 October 1642, which was a Sunday. This didn't please the Puritans in the Roundhead ranks, because Sunday was a day for going to church, not for fighting. That's exactly what the Earl of Essex was doing when he first learnt that the enemy royalist forces were gathering on Edge Hill. Essex apologized to the vicar, then gathered his men at the foot of the hill.

THE FIRST SHOT IS FIRED

The first shot of the first battle of the English Civil War was fired by Essex's Roundheads at three o'clock. The Cavaliers fired back . . . and not a lot happened apart from some frantic reloading. It's not that both sides were bad shots or anything. It's just that the two sides were quite far apart and the long-barrelled guns they were firing (called muskets) didn't have a very long range, and weren't very accurate. Still, there were some impressive bangs and puffs of smoke, and at least the fighting had officially *started*.

CHARGE!

The royalist Cavaliers had a distinct advantage in that they were charging downhill. The Roundheads were literally fighting an uphill battle, but they had more men. The Roundhead cavalry made a mess of things and had to turn and flee from the Cavalier cavalry, which left the rows of musketeers exposed. It's not much good facing a horde of stamping horses if you're only armed with a cumbersome rifle, but things were easier for the Roundhead pikemen. They were armed with sharp, pointy pikes which were just the thing for jabbing into horses and riders alike. Soon it was the Cavalier cavalry's turn to try to retreat . . . uphill. Now, as they rode off they could be shot at.

WE WON! NO, WE WON!

Although the Roundheads managed to take the royal standard off the Cavaliers – which was a big embarrassment for the royalists because it was a symbol of the king's authority to rally around – no one seemed quite sure what to do next. Everyone was exhausted, and no one was too thrilled to be fighting fellow countrymen. (There were no women fighting, remember.) Although both armies had a core of professional, trained soldiers, most Cavaliers and Roundheads were just ordinary people called up to fight: 'tapsters' and 'town-apprentices' Cromwell called his men. Not only that, there were no distinctive uniforms to tell each side apart. The only easy way to tell a royalist from a Roundhead was the colour of his sash . . . and sashes could fall off or get covered in mud, and you didn't really want to kill one of your mates by mistake. None of this made the Battle of Edgehill any fun. (And if you're still wondering what a tapster is, I think it was someone who worked in a pub.)

TO LONDON . . . EVENTUALLY

On Monday 24 October, Essex led his Roundhead army away from the battlefield and headed off to London. There, with the help of not just men this time, but women and children too – about 100,000 people in total – they built defences against the king: forts, ditches and a few other nasty surprises. When the Cavaliers finally turned up, in 1643, they only got as far as a place called Turnham Green . . . and seeing all those defences was certainly enough to turn 'em green! (OK, OK. It's a terrible pun, but it was too good an opportunity to miss.) They simply gave up and headed for Oxford, without a single pike being prodded or musket being fired. But I'm getting ahead of myself again . . .

FROM CAPTAIN TO COLONEL

Oliver Cromwell spent the first few months of 1643 whipping up support for the Roundhead cause in the Fen country in and around his home county. He seized what he could from the royalists to give to the parliamentarian cause, and was eager to recruit religious men to fight as Roundheads, because he was convinced that they'd fight with commitment and honour. Soon after, he was promoted to colonel. Cambridge became a garrison town – a town where troops were permanently housed and ready for action. The town's defences were strengthened, and new fortifications added.

THE UPPER HAND

Oliver led his men to many victories. His troops stood head and shoulders above the rest. I don't mean they were taller than the average Roundhead soldier or that they wore high heels, I mean that their skill and discipline made them stand out as excellent men. Drawn from (in alphabetical order, to avoid accusations of favouritism) Cambridgeshire, Essex, Hertfordshire, Norfolk and Suffolk, they became known as the Eastern Association and there were 20,000 of them. Our Oliver was now a very important man indeed.

TROUBLE IN YORK

The biggest and bloodiest battle of the Civil War took place near the city of York in 1644. A Cavalier leader, the Marquis of Newcastle, and 6,000 of his men were besieged in the city. Besieged meant that York was surrounded by parliamentarians who decided who could go in and who could come out. The answer to the latter was NO ONE. The parliamentarian forces included Yorkshiremen under Lord Fairfax, associated counties (including those under Oliver Cromwell), and Scots. Yes, Scots. In January, about 21,000 Scotsmen had marched into England via Berwick to support the Roundhead cause, in different parts of the country.

RUPERT TO THE RESCUE!

At the end of June 1644, an army of Cavaliers streamed over the hills from Lancashire to free Newcastle and his men. This royalist army was led by Prince Rupert of Bavaria, nicknamed the 'Prince of Plunder' and 'Prince Robber' by the Roundheads. He was King Charles I's nephew and it was he who'd led the Cavaliers at the Battle of Edgehill too. When news reached those surrounding York that the enemy were on the way, they pulled out and lined up ready to face them on the moor of Long Marston.

PREPARE TO FIGHT!

Rupert got around them by crossing the River Ouse. He freed Newcastle (the man) from York (the city) and there it could have ended: a great Cavalier victory. Instead, Prince Rupert and Newcastle joined forces and went to face the Roundheads. The result? The battle of Marston Moor, fought, some say, in just three hours – 7pm to 10pm, in case you were wondering – on Tuesday 2 July 1644. The reason the battle began so late was because, just as Rupert thought he'd feed his men and fight the following morning, and the Marquis of Newcastle slunk off for a snooze, Oliver Cromwell sent in the Ironsides.

THE IRONSIDES

The Ironsides were Oliver Cromwell's cavalry, the most feared bunch of soldiers in the Civil War. They themselves were said to fear no one, except God. They didn't drink and they didn't swear (and drinking and swearing were usually the most popular pastimes of ordinary soldiers). It's rather romantically suggested that they were never beaten in any battle they fought.

THE BLOODIEST OF BATTLES

When the Cavaliers least expected it, Oliver's Roundhead cavalry charged. But, surprise or no surprise, Prince Rupert hadn't earned the name Prince Plunder for nothing and soon retaliated, taking a serious chunk out of the Roundhead army. But Cromwell's forces, supported by the Scots, were too much for him. In the light of day – as opposed to the light of night because, the truth be told, it was pretty bright because there was a full moon – it was discovered over 3,000 Cavaliers were dead or soon would be. Plenty more were injured. Oliver claimed that 'of 20,000 the prince hath not 4,000 left'. At best, this was a gross exaggeration. At worst it was a whopping great fib. Whatever the figures, this was a great victory for the Roundheads and for Oliver Cromwell. Speaking of the fallen foe, Oliver said, 'God made them as stubble to our swords' . . . which might possibly be a joke about shaving, which is, in itself, hardly surprising when you were taught by a man called Dr Beard.

DEATHS IN THE FAMILY

It was Oliver's less pleasant task to write to his sister Margaret's husband, telling them of the death of their eldest son at the battle. He reported that God had taken him away 'by a cannon-shot'. It shattered his leg, which they then had to cut off . . . and the boy died. It's also thought, by those who know such things, that Oliver's own son Oliver – the no-ice-cream-jokes cornet, back on page 30, remember? – died at about this time too. Not at Marston Moor but at a place called Knaresborough.

AFTER MARSTON MOOR

The first thing to happen after the battle was the Roundheads' capture of York, but not everything went their way. In September 1644, the Cavaliers managed to force Essex and the Roundheads out of Devon into Fowey in Cornwall . . . which is surrounded by the sea on three out of four sides. The only hope was that reinforcements would arrive by water. In those days, ships were dependent on wind power and boats on oar power (or muscle), and both were dependent on the weather. There were plenty of troops waiting to sail round to help their leader, but their ships were blown back the way they came! Essex himself escaped on a ship and his cavalry escaped on horseback, but the poor old Roundhead foot soldiers were taken prisoner.

THE PROBLEM WITH PRISONERS

Someone very clever once said that an army marches on its stomach, which may not be side-splittingly funny or literally true – an army marches on its feet – but it's a good point. If you don't feed your soldiers, they get all thin and weedy and can't lift their

weapons. King Charles was discovering that you had to feed prisoners too. When he'd first heard reports that 6,000 Roundheads were now in his custody he was pleased. He thought things such as 'That'll show 'em!' and 'See? We're not such a pushover, now, are we?' Then it dawned on him that food that could be going to HIS men now had to go to feed the enemy . . . so he let them go. But he kept their weapons, so at least he'd got something out of it!

THE YEAR'S END

On 27 October 1644, there was another one of those indecisive battles when it's not really clear which side, if either, won. Called the Second Battle of Newbury, it's important for another reason. Oliver Cromwell thought that his boss, the Earl of Manchester, hadn't tried hard enough. In fact, he reckoned that if Manchester had been more vigorous, the Second Battle of Newbury could have been a Roundhead victory instead of a draw. On 25

November, Cromwell got up in the House of Commons and said as much. He went even further when, on Wednesday 9 December, he suggested that the Roundhead army needed to be completely remodelled.

THE NEW MODEL ARMY

On 3 April of the following year (1645), both Houses of Parliament finally passed something called the 'Self-denying Ordinance'. This stated that members of parliament couldn't also be military commanders. Suddenly, Essex (who'd deserted his men in Cornwall) and Manchester (whom our Oliver had been so quick to criticize) were out of a job. Manchester was given a new role with a flashy title and Essex was given a pension. (In other words, they promised him a lot of money if he went quietly. As it was, he was dead within a couple of years so parliament didn't actually have to pay out that much.) Now the army could be developed on proper lines. It would be a 'model' army, as in a fine example, not 'model' as in one made up of toy soldiers, OK?

AN EXCEPTIONAL EXCEPTION

Self-denying Ordinance or no Self-denying Ordinance, Oliver was obviously the man to lead the Roundhead army against Prince Rupert . . . so parliament simply gave him a special dispensation. In other words, it was agreed that Cromwell was a special case and that the Self-denying Ordinance could be ignored. (This is the one-rule-for-him-another-rule-for-someone-else way of doing things, popular with rulers and governments the world over.) Cromwell not only routed Rupert at Islip Bridge (which is near Oxford), he also led his troops to victory at Radcot Bridge. In June 1645, Oliver was made second in command of the 'New Model Army' under Sir Thomas Fairfax, its general-in-chief. His title was lieutenant-general. Later that month, he took 6,000 hand-picked horsemen to join Fairfax in Northampton.

THE BATTLE OF NASEBY

On 14 June, royalist and parliamentary forces faced each other at Naseby, Northamptonshire. Prince Rupert was there, as usual, but this time so was the king in person. For once, the Cavalier cavalry seemed to get the upper hand over Oliver's Roundhead cavalry, but not for long. Charles I – being either very brave or very foolhardy, which is a polite way of saying stupid – decided to charge into the enemy ranks. A quick-thinking Cavalier, who realized that his king would be squashed flat, shot or stabbed in less than a minute, grabbed the bridle of Charles's horse. He then began leading the horse (with the king on it) away to safety. Seeing their king apparently retreat, the Cavaliers took this as a signal to do the same. Naseby suddenly turned into the royalists' most humiliating defeat!

SUCCESS AFTER SUCCESS

In March, Cromwell defeated a new 'enemy' at Shaftsbury, called the Clubmen. These started out as a group of ordinary folk who were fed up being stuck in the middle. They didn't like paying the taxes parliament raised to fight the king, and they didn't like the king for . . . well, for all the annoying things he'd done. As far as Cromwell was concerned, if you weren't *for* the Roundheads, you were *against* them. So he sorted them out. In September, he then took Bristol from the royalists with Fairfax.

AN END IN SIGHT?

After a quiet period, with the king keeping a low profile, Cromwell returned to parliament in April 1646. He was unhappy with the way that the Presbyterian MPs were behaving, so he sided with a group of independent MPs and spoke his mind! The Presbyterians had been getting more and more powerful in parliament and, Oliver

thought, far too big for their boots. That was on the 22nd. On the 27th, the king rode out of Oxford – a royalist stronghold under siege from the Roundheads – in disguise and headed towards the Scottish army. Charles I had got it into his head that they might offer him protection . . . and they did!

THE SKITTISH SCOTS

Many Scots were Presbyterians and, so long as the English Presbyterians had influence and power over the English Parliament and Roundhead forces, the Scots were pretty happy to support these groups . . . but now that the English Presbyterians were losing their grip, Charles looked like he might make a useful

ally instead. Of course, they'd have to convince him to become a Presbyterian himself and to turn England into a Presbyterian country if he won the war, but it might just work . . .

CHANGING SIDES

In a way, Charles was a sort-of-prisoner of the Scots but, at the same time, under their protection as a sort-of-guest. The Scots kept on trying to convince him to convert to being a Presbyterian, but he refused. If he'd agreed (which was very unlikely) the war might have ended there and then. As it was, they sold him back to the English Parliament for a staggering £400,000, on the understanding that they went straight home once they'd handed him over! This they did in February 1647.

IMPORTANT OCCASIONS

15 June 1646 was an important date for Oliver Cromwell, but it had little to do with the Civil War. This was the day that his daughter Bridget married Henry Ireton, a commissionary general to Sir Thomas Fairfax, Oliver's boss. It was five days later, on Saturday 20 June, that a treaty was signed between the Roundhead forces and nearby Oxford and the royalists allowed to leave unharmed. Now, this *was* an important historical date. It marked the end of the First Civil War.

THE FIGHT CONTINUES

The end of the First Civil War wasn't the end of the fighting. The truth be told, lots of people clump all the civil wars together and count them as one big one nowadays – because, you guessed it, calling this one the *First* Civil War hints that there was another one on its way. The First Civil War had been Roundheads against Cavaliers, in other words royalist against parliamentarian. Although that was still the clear divide in the Second Civil War, there was much more in-fighting too. There were now power struggles within parliamentary forces and splinter – ouch! – groups trying to put forward their own ideas, or to force them on others. June 1647 saw a big demonstration against the Presbyterian majority in the House of Commons, and was followed by Fairfax and Cromwell's New Model Army marching on London!

WHERE'S OUR PAY?

Since the 'defeat' of the Cavaliers, parliament hadn't been sure what to do with their New Model Army. Here were 20,000 or so men (perhaps even 30,000) with very little to do. 12,000 were sent to Ireland to keep an eye on the poor old Catholics over there and to make life difficult for them . . . but what about the rest? They were discontented as it was, and had every reason to be. These were the men who'd brought parliament victory, but they hadn't been paid for over 40 weeks! When some units were disbanded they received some pay, but the soldiers seized this in part payment for their missing wages and still demanded the rest.

THE MARCH ON LONDON

Slowly but surely, the army began to march to London. On 10 June, a letter signed by, amongst others, Fairfax and Oliver Cromwell was sent to the Lord Mayor of London. In it, they made it clear that the army 'desire no alteration to the civil government' and warned Londoners against taking up arms against them, saying that they freed themselves 'from all that ruin which may befall that great and populous city; having thereby washed our hands thereof'. In other words: mess with us, and we won't be responsible for the consequences!

MARTIAL RULE

Despite the fine words about not changing parliament, of course that's exactly what the army went and did. They threw in jail those people they disagreed with, and told the remaining members to vote to give them all that back pay or else. A new group had sprung up (outside parliament) called the Levellers. They suggested that parliament should be scrapped and England start again with a new constitution. They also recommended other remarkable ideas such as one person one vote and that – hold on to your hats – included WOMEN. They thought there should be an agreement between the people and those who governed on their behalf, called the Contract of the People. Oliver and others considered these ideas . . . but decided against them.

THAT SNEAKY STUART

Since 8 August 1647, the king had been a virtual prisoner in Hampton Court. In other words he was under house arrest. He could do what he liked in the palace, but he mustn't leave it. But that's exactly what he did. The Roundheads guessed that he'd sneaked back to see the Scots again, but what they hadn't guessed was that the meeting place wasn't Scotland, but the Isle of Wight. He promised to make England and Ireland Presbyterian if only the Scots would help him get England back . . . and if he didn't have to be Presbyterian himself!

THAT SECOND CIVIL WAR

In January 1648, parliament agreed that no one should try to arrange any more treaties or agreement with the king. He was a lost cause. That same month, Cromwell suppressed a group of soldiers who mutinied in support of the Levellers. In spring, the Second Civil War – or *Civil War II: The Sequel* – broke out. Uprisings in key cities such as London and Canterbury were put down and Cromwell marched his men to Wales to quash – now there's a good word – a rebellion there. In May, he took Chepstow and, in July, Pembroke Castle surrendered to him. Then it was on to face the Scottish forces. Now Oliver Cromwell was winning victory after victory after victory. He entered Edinburgh, he took Carlisle. Then he returned to London in December where parliament thanked him for all he'd done.

PRIDE'S PURGE

December 1648 saw another big shake-up in parliament. The army still had a stranglehold over the place with guards on the door. One such man, a Colonel Pride, prevented any Presbyterian members from going in, for fear that they might vote to do a deal with the king who was making all the right noises about turning England into a Presbyterian country. 140 of them were arrested! The 60 members left were called the Rump Parliament. (You'll find out why very soon.) Now the minority of independent MPs in parliament suddenly found themselves the ruling majority . . . and plans to put the king on trial went underway.

CHARLES GETS THE CHOP

How you felt about what happened next very much depended on whose side you were on. In January 1649, the king was brought to the High Court three times to answer the charges against him (and our Oliver was there on two occasions). Refusing to recognize the right of the court to do what it was doing, he refused to plead guilty, not guilty or anything. His enemies say that this was undignified, haughty and typical. His supporters say he was just being dignified and regal. Either way, he was found guilty of High Treason, his death warrant was signed by 60 (with Oliver's name fourth on the list) and he was executed on 30 January 1649. If this book was called *GET A LIFE! Charles I*, I'd tell you lots of gory details, but it isn't. So move along now, please. There's nothing to see.

LONG LIVE THE REPUBLIC!

By May, England was a republic. It had no monarch and was ruled by parliament. In fact, this was the remains of the same Long Parliament that the king himself had summoned way back on page 22 . . . except that there was no House of Lords now. There was just a House of Commons made up of the 'rump' of 60 remaining members and nicknamed the Rump Parliament. Rump means 'buttocks' (so we can have a good giggle) but it also means leftovers, which is what this parliament was made up of. This period of history when England was ruled without a monarch was called the Commonwealth.

CROMWELL AND THE CELTS

However fair and honourable Oliver Cromwell liked to make himself out to be, his treatment of the Irish shows him in a very bad light. Made a member of the new Council of State in February 1649, he was declared Lord-Lieutenant of Ireland in March and landed in Dublin on 15 August. There had been a Catholic rebellion which had been blowing hot and cold for the past eight years. For someone who was supposed to be God-fearing and humble, he had his 12,000 troops do terrible, stomach-churning things to Catholic clergymen, landowners and soldiers, plus – no doubt – a few ordinary men, women and children along the way. Having killed over 2,600 people, he declared the country Protestant and returned to England in May 1650. Parliament was so delighted by what he'd done, they made him 'Captain-General', the commander-in-chief of all Commonwealth forces. Between June 1650 and August 1651, Oliver turned his attention to crushing the Scots, who were still a thorn in the Roundheads' side. Despite a serious illness in Glasgow in spring 1651, he was a rip-roaring 'success' there too.

THE KING IS DEAD. LONG LIVE THE KING

Charles I was dead, but the monarchy wasn't. His son, later to become Charles II, was hiding out in Scotland. At the Battle of Dunbar, on 3 September 1650, the royalist Scottish forces were crushed by Cromwell's army. Over 3,000 died and 10,000 were captured. And how many men did Oliver Cromwell lose? Just 28, as in 'two less than 30'!!! On 1 January 1651, the Scots crowned Charles II 'King of England, Scotland and Ireland', but only after they'd put aside a day for 'humiliation for the sins of the royal family'. Down in England, the Roundheads called him 'Charlie the Pretender'. There was no room for a king in the Commonwealth.

OLIVER'S FINEST HOUR

In August 1651, Charles II and a new batch of Scottish troops marched into England. When he and his troops reached Worcester, they waited. Cromwell and his army were

marching to meet them. On 3 September 1651, exactly a year to the day after the king's defeat at Dunbar, the Battle of Worcester was fought. Charles only had 12,000 men. Cromwell had closer to 30,000. No prizes for guessing who won this one. Charles was last seen slinking off back to town, then hiding up a tree. Perhaps there'll be a *GET A LIFE!* book about him one day. Who knows? This battle marked the end of the Second Civil War.

THE LORD PROTECTOR
(WITH NOT THAT MANY PAGES TO GO)

The following year, 1652, Oliver Cromwell was 53 years old and probably the most powerful man in England, if not Britain. In January, the government of Scotland had been taken over by English Commissioners so (however reluctantly) England and Scotland were united as one nation. In 1653, some members of 'the rump' of the Long Parliament – yes, it was still going – decided that it would be a jolly good idea if they passed an act making themselves members for life. In other words, these people would be governing the nation until they dropped dead! Oliver had other ideas and made a pretty amazing speech . . .

THE END OF THE LONG PARLIAMENT

He started by praising its members for 'their pains and care of the public good' but soon began criticizing them for their 'self interest and other faults'. Then he began slapping his hat in his hand like a tambourine and stamping his foot in rage. If that wasn't bad enough, he started calling some of them drunkards and cried, 'I say you are no parliament!' Oliver then grabbed the mace – like a giant sceptre, it was the symbol of the authority of parliament – and handed it to a musketeer. Who would dare argue with this man? He had the mightiest army the country had seen under his command, and a number of musketeers (men with muskets!) at his side. The Long Parliament was well and truly at an end after 12-and-a-half years.

COME ON DOWN!

Now a new parliament was needed and Cromwell, as 'Captain-General and Commander-in-Chief', sent summons to those few people he wished to serve as its members. On what authority he did this isn't altogether clear. What is clear, though, is that Oliver had emerged from the Civil Wars as the Big Cheese/Top Dog/Main Man/Number One Guy. This new parliament was called the Little Parliament or *Barebone's Parliament*, because it was stripped to its bare essentials, with 140 members 'of approved fidelity and honesty' . . . and you can't strip much further than your bare bones. It met on 4 July 1653.

SPEECH! SPEECH!

In his speech to this new parliament, Oliver laid out his plans for the nation. He tried to make himself out to be a man of the people, but was more than a little embarrassed that he'd got rid of the old parliament like a king would . . . and was treating this new parliament as his own, like a king would too! It seemed to be a case of don't judge me by what I do now, but by what I *say*! Ho hum.

IN THE INTEREST OF THE NATION

On Friday 2 December 1653, this parliament reported that it no longer existed for the good of the Commonwealth and promptly resigned to Cromwell (whom they referred to as the Lord General). They then proceeded to give *him* the law-making powers he'd given them. Oliver Cromwell called a Council of Officers and other key figures 'in the interest of the nation' to decide what to do next. There was much excitement at the news.

THE LORD PROTECTOR

Now Oliver accepted the rather grand title of Lord Protector of the Commonwealth of England, Scotland and Ireland. His 'ceremony of installation' took place in Westminster Hall on 16 December 1653. He wore a plain black suit of rich velvet with matching cloak and hat.

Around the hat was a thick gold band. He must have looked very impressive.

WARTS AND ALL

At a time when most official portraits were ridiculously flattering – with a person who looked like a wart hog in real life being painted to appear like a god – Oliver Cromwell's approach was most refreshing. He instructed the artist to paint his 'pimples, warts and everything as you see me'. And Oliver did indeed have a few lumps and bumps: a huge one above his right eye, and one above his chin. He also had a rather big head for his body and a rather big nose for his head. He was certainly no oil painting . . . if you see what I mean.

NEW HOPE

On 3 September 1654 – the anniversary of the victories at Dunbar and at Worcester – Oliver's first Protectorate Parliament sat, with 400 members for England, 340 for Scotland and 30 for Ireland, after the first election in fourteen years. The following day, Oliver rode in state from Whitehall to the Abbey Church in Westminster. He was the first commoner ever to rule England.

HOLDING THE REINS OF POWER

Oliver Cromwell remained ruler for the rest of his life. (He died at the ripe old age – for those days – of 59 in 1658.) He owed much of his strength to the army, which remained loyal to him to the end. He also relied on the power of the land owners (or 'gentry') but was sure to keep them and the army apart, so they couldn't get together and realize that they could get on fine without him, thank you very much. Life wasn't plain sailing, though. He dissolved parliament in January 1655, and appointed ten major-generals to be pretty much responsible for the running of day-to-day affairs. When a new parliament was formed in September 1657, Oliver Cromwell barred over 100 members whom he decided were 'unsuitable'. And what *he* said went!

KING? NOT THE DONE THING!

In April 1657, a large majority of the House of Commons urged Oliver to accept the role and title of king. This was not only the very greatest honour they could think of giving him, but it also meant that the Cromwells would become the new royal family and his descendants kings after him. Oliver refused but, following the end of the rule of the major generals, under an act passed in June, he was allowed to name his successor to rule after him and to create a House of Lords too. With sweeping powers like that, who needed to be king anyway?

A PURITAN NATION

There's been plenty about battles and parliaments and kings hiding up trees - well, OK, one king up one tree - but what was life like for ordinary people in Commonwealth England? The main building in any village was the church, and in any city its cathedral. These buildings would have towered above everything around them and been the centre of the community . . . and now they looked different. Many'd had their statues torn down or defaced. (These were considered 'monuments of Papist idolatry' and had no place in the Puritan world.) Stained glass windows were replaced with sensible, Puritan plain glass ones! Inside, the religious services were simple and serious too. Christmas Day became a 'fast day', with no eating allowed! There were no celebrations. In fact, soldiers spent Christmas morning searching Londoners' kitchens and seizing any meat they found being prepared . . . the spoilsports!

THE GOOSE STEP

There's a nursery rhyme which begins 'Goosey, Goosey gander/Where shall I wander?' but the goosey it's referring to isn't a bird. It's talking about the goose step, which was the way Cromwell's soldiers marched like scissors, bringing their feet almost up to knee height. The rhyme ends 'There I met an old man/Who would not say his prayers./I took him by the left

leg/And threw him down the stairs.' The meaning there is plain enough. If you didn't pray in the way you were supposed to pray, things could turn out very nastily for you.

NOT ALWAYS MR POPULAR

A number of attempts were made to remove Oliver Cromwell from office, or to kill him. Being such a powerful man, he was bound to attract enemies and there were a number of royalist plots against him. John Gerard, Peter Vowell, Sir Henry Slingsby and John Hewit are the names of just a few people who were executed for their trouble. Others were transported to the West Indies for lives of hard labour.

WAR ABROAD

Just because there'd been civil war and sweeping changes at home, didn't mean to say that the new England had stayed out of foreign affairs. In 1655, Oliver Cromwell intervened on behalf of the Protestants being persecuted in the valleys of Piedmont. In 1656, the English admiral Blake – not to be confused with the much earlier Drake – did much to stop piracy on British ships in the Mediterranean, and told the Catholic countries to stop interfering with British commerce on the seas. From 1655-8, England was even at war with Spain, with Admiral Blake winning a great victory off Cadiz. In June 1658, Dunkirk was surrendered to English forces and came under English rule.

DEATH OF A DAUGHTER

1658 saw the death of Oliver Cromwell's favourite daughter, on 6 August. Elizabeth (named after her mother) died at 3 o'clock in the morning at Hampton Court. According to an eye-witness, she'd been in a great deal of pain and had 'frequent convulsion fits'. She was about 29 years old.

Although he took comfort from his religious beliefs, Oliver was very saddened and badly affected by her death.

OFF TO MEET HIS MAKER

Oliver himself couldn't really have picked a more suitable date for his own death if he'd tried. He too died in 1658, four weeks or so after Elizabeth, on 3 September. Those of you with beady eyes and good memories will realize that this was the very date that was the anniversary of his victory at Dunbar, his glorious victory at Worcester and the historical opening of the First Protectorate Parliament! He had been unwell for some time, and Elizabeth's death hadn't helped matters. As Oliver lay dying, he named his successor. The next Lord Protector would be his son Richard. Why choose him of all his sons? Because he was the only one left.

A FEW LOOSE ENDS

And there our story should end, because this is *GET A LIFE! Oliver Cromwell* and Oliver's life is over. England didn't remain a Commonwealth much longer. His son Richard – nicknamed Tumbledown Dick – was useless and the army restless. Less than two years later, on 29 May 1660, King Charles II marched into London with over 100,000 people. The monarchy was back in Britain . . . and is still here, the last time I checked. But Oliver's story isn't quite over yet . . .

A GRAVE DECISION

The victorious royalists (no one was really calling them Cavaliers any more) wanted to *punish* someone for what had happened to Charles II's poor old dad, Charles I, and to the country. The ideal person to pin the blame on would have been Oliver Cromwell himself. Boy, would they have loved to have hanged him or beheaded him . . . so, dead or not, they decided to do *both* anyway. They dug up his coffin, took out the body, hanged him, cut him down and then chopped off his head. How very civilized. 'God Save The King!'

TIMELINE,
at home and abroad

1599	Oliver Cromwell is born.
	Shakespeare and friends build the Globe Theatre in London.
1600	*Recorder music becomes all the rage.*
1616	Cromwell goes to Cambridge.
1620	*Inventor Cornelius van Drebbel builds a submarine!*
1628	Cromwell becomes an MP.
1630	*Work starts on building the Taj Mahal in Agra, India.*
1640	Long Parliament first sits.
1642	First Civil War begins.
	Battle of Edgehill.
	Cromwell creates Ironsides.
1644	Battle of Marston Moor.
1645	Battle of Naseby.
	Surrender of royalist Winchester to Cromwell.
	End of First Civil War.
1648	Second Civil War begins.
1649	King Charles I executed at Whitehall.
1650	*People in Britain begin drinking cups of tea.*
1651	Cromwell defeats Charles II and Worcester.
	Second Civil War ends.
1653	Cromwell ends Long Parliament.
	Cromwell proclaimed 'Lord Protector'.
1657	*Drinking chocolate arrives in England!*
1658	Cromwell dies.